SPIRITUAL DISCIPLINES

STUDY &
MEDITATION

BIBLE STUDIES

Jan Johnson

6 STUDIES WITH NOTES FOR LEADERS

ivp

InterVarsity Press
Downers Grove, Illinois
Leicester, England

InterVarsity Press
P.O. Box 1400, Downers Grove, IL 60515-1426
World Wide Web: www.ivpress.com
E-mail: mail@ivpress.com

Inter-Varsity Press, England
38 De Montfort Street, Leicester LE1 7GP, England
World Wide Web: www.ivpbooks.com
E-mail: ivp@uccf.org.uk

InterVarsity Press® is the book-publishing division of InterVarsity Christian Fellowship/USA®, a student movement active on campus at hundreds of universities, colleges and schools of nursing in the United States of America, and a member movement of the International Fellowship of Evangelical Students. For information about local and regional activities, write Public Relations Dept., InterVarsity Christian Fellowship/USA, 6400 Schroeder Rd., P.O. Box 7895, Madison, WI 53707-7895, or visit the IVCF website at <www.ivcf.org>.

Inter-Varsity Press, England, is the book-publishing division of the Universities and Colleges Christian Fellowship (formerly the Inter-Varsity Fellowship), a student movement linking Christian Unions in universities and colleges throughout the United Kingdom and the Republic of Ireland, and a member movement of the International Fellowship of Evangelical Students. For information about local and national activities write to UCCF, 38 De Montfort Street, Leicester LE1 7GP.

Cover design: Cindy Kiple

Cover and interior image: Digital Vision

U.S. ISBN 0-8308-2091-4

U.K. ISBN 0-85111-698-1

Printed in the United States of America ∞

P	22	21	20	19	18	17	16	15	14	13	12	11	10	9	8	7	6	5	4	3	2	1
Y	20	19	18	17	16	15	14	13	12	11	10	09	08	07	06	05	04	03				

CONTENTS

INTRODUCING

Study & Meditation

Have you ever wondered how God changes people? Maybe it seems as if old habits never change no matter how hard you try. Maybe you've become discouraged with your lack of growth into Christlikeness. You know that you are forgiven through Jesus' suffering on the cross, and you realize that you are totally accepted by God on that basis. This is wonderful. And yet your desire to live in a way that pleases God somehow constantly falls short of the mark.

God desires to transform our souls. This transformation occurs as we recognize that God created us to live in an interactive relationship with the Trinity. Our task is not to transform ourselves, but to stay connected with God in as much of life as possible. As we pay attention to the nudges of the Holy Spirit, we become disciples of Christ. Our task is to do the connecting, while God does the perfecting.

As we connect with God, we gradually begin acting more like Christ. We become more likely to weep over our enemies instead of discrediting them. We're more likely to give up power instead of taking control. We're more likely to point out another's successes rather than grab the credit. Connecting with God changes us on the inside, and we slowly become the tenderhearted, conscientious people our families always wished we'd become. This transformation of our souls through the work of the Holy Spirit results in "Christ in you, the hope of glory" (Colossians 1:27).

God does in us what we cannot do by trying to be good. Trying to be good generally makes us obnoxious because it's so obvious that we're only trying. The goodness doesn't come from within ourselves. When we do succeed at being good, we subtly look down on those who don't do as well. Either way, we remain focused on self instead of on setting our hearts on things above.

Connecting with God, then, is important. But what does connecting with God look like? Through the work of the Holy Spirit, we copy Jesus in behind-the-scenes, everyday activities he did to connect with God. As we let these activities become habits, we slowly become "trained" to have the heart of Christ and behave as he did. These activities are spiritual disciplines, also called spiritual exercises or strategies.

How Spiritual Disciplines Work

We connect with God through spiritual disciplines or exercises. Study and meditation, the topics of these Bible studies, are two of them. Other disciplines include solitude, silence, worship, celebration, prayer, listening, service, secrecy, reflection, confession, fasting, simplicity, community and submission. These exercises are studied in the other Spiritual Disciplines Bible Studies. Still other disciplines can be used, some of which are written about in the classics of the faith and others God will show you. Henri Nouwen said that a spiritual discipline is anything that helps us practice "how to become attentive to that small voice and willing to respond when we hear it."[*]

---

[*]Sources for quoted material can be found at the end of the guide.

How do spiritual disciplines help us connect with God?

- They build our relationship with God as we acquaint ourselves with the ways of God. (It's possible, of course, to do these disciplines in a legalistic way and never bond with Christ.)

- They build our trust in Christ. Some of the disciplines are uncomfortable. You have to go out on a limb. You try fasting, and you don't die. You serve someone, and it turns out to be fun and enriching.

- They force us to make "little decisions" that multiply. Your little decision to abstain from watching a television show helps you to deny yourself and love others in all sorts of ways.

- They reorganize our impulses so that obedience is more natural. For example, if you have a spiritual discipline of practicing the presence of God, you may learn to automatically pray the breath prayer "Into thy hands" when someone opposes you. Without your realizing it, your opponent is no longer an adversary, but a person God is dealing with or perhaps even speaking through in some way.

- They help us eventually behave like Christ—but this is by God's miraculous work, not our direct effort.

- They teach us to trust that God will do the work in our inner being through the power of the Spirit (Ephesians 3:16). Your spirituality is not about you; it's the work of God in you. You get to cooperate in God's "family business" of transforming the world.

How We Get Spiritual Disciplines Wrong

Spiritual exercises must be done with the goal of connecting, not for any sake of their own or any desire to check them off a list of "to do" items. If you read your Bible just to get it done, or because you've heard this will help you have a better day, you'll be anxious to complete the Bible study questions or to get to the bottom of the page of today's reading. But if your goal in Bible reading is to connect with God, you may pause whenever you sense God speaking to you. You'll stop and meditate on it. You may pray certain phrases back to God, indicating your needs or your wishes or your questions. You may choose to read that passage day after day for a month because God keeps using it to speak to you.

After such a session, you will have a stronger desire to connect with God. That "little choice" you made to connect will leave you slightly different for life.

The exercise or discipline is beneficial because it helps you practice connecting with God. If you want to play the piano well or swing a tennis racket well, you have to practice certain exercises over and over. Good baseball players train behind the scenes by practicing their batting day after day, with no crowds watching.[*] That's what spiritual disciplines or exercises are about. If you can hear God in Bible study and meditation, you'll more likely hear God in a board meeting or an altercation with a recalcitrant teen when passions run high. In life with God, we get good at connecting on an everyday basis by devoting time to developing the skills needed.

The Disciplines of Bible Study and Meditation

The techniques of Bible study are familiar to many—observing the facts of Scripture, interpreting it in light of its historical and biblical context, and thinking of ways to put it into practice. Meditation on Scripture, however, is very different. Here's a comparison.

---

[*]This comparison originated from and is expanded in Dallas Willard, *The Spirit of the Disciplines* (San Francisco: Harper & Row, 1988), p. 3.

In the Study Method, You . . .	In the Meditation Method, You . . .
dissect the text	savor the text and enter into it
ask questions about the text	let the text ask questions of you
read and compare facts and new ways of applying facts	read to let God speak to you (in light of facts already absorbed)

The Bible doesn't instruct us on how to meditate for the same reason it doesn't instruct us on how to fast. These were common spiritual disciplines of the day that folks already knew how to do, or they knew other folks who did. Through the ages, the mechanics of meditation have been kept alive mostly through monastic communities. The two most common methods of meditation are presented in sessions 5-6.

Bible study is an excellent way of setting oneself up for meditation because through it you come to understand the main point of the Scripture. Still, study does not rule meditation. God may help you choose an obscure word in the passage to ponder or point out a sideline character for you to identify with. Each time you meditate on the passage, it's likely to be different because you will be in a different set of circumstances.

How Do These Studies Work?

The studies in this guide examine reasons to study and meditate, their effects, and how to do them. Each session includes several elements.

Turning Toward God presents discussion or reflection questions and exercises to draw us into the topic at hand.

Hearing God Through the Word draws us into a study of a related passage of Scripture with questions that connect it to life and invite us to reflect on what God is saying.

Transformation Exercises are activities or thoughts to experiment with in order to experience the spiritual exercise studied. At the end of the study, look at these exercises and choose the one that fits you best, according to your personality or your current needs. Think of a time to try it on your own, and report back to the group the following week.

Perhaps you'll read the exercise and think it's too elementary or too difficult for you. Adapt it as needed. Or maybe you think you can guess what you'll experience, so you don't have to do it. The point is to experience it. Go ahead and try.

Using These Studies in Retreats

These studies work well for an individual taking a personal retreat. Simply do the studies at your own pace, and do not rush them. Allow enough time to do the transformation exercises as well. Don't feel you have to do all the studies. In fact, you may wish to focus only on one discipline and use only those studies.

A group wishing to explore certain disciplines can also use one of these studies the same way. Be sure to allow time for participants to do the transformation exercises. Some exercises may be done as a group. Others may be done individually, with group members reporting back to each other about how they heard God during the exercise.

For either type of retreat, allow plenty of time for pondering. May these studies help you move a few steps closer to living your life in union with God.

1

IMMERSING YOURSELF IN GOD'S THOUGHTS

DEUTERONOMY 6:1-9

Dead words on a page. That's how folks often approach Bible reading and study. So they long for an "exciting" teacher to make the words "come alive."

Yet the words of Scripture have been God-breathed (2 Timothy 3:16). God uses them to connect with us and communicate to us what genuine goodness is. Inhaling these carefully breathed words of life can transform us into radically different people who think as God thinks and love as God loves.

Bible study, then, involves more than examination of facts. It's a communication of who God is and an immersion into God's counsel for living wisely. Each day as we read God's Word, God imparts to us a little more of what we need to know. We can look forward to hearing from God every day as we read Scripture.

Turning Toward God

If you were to read the Bible today mostly out of a sense of obligation—hoping to finish the day's reading quickly or simply to get it done—how would this help you or not help you?

Hearing God Through the Word

In today's passage, Moses reviews God's directives for the nation of Israel so they can live a life of wholeness and goodness as they enter the Promised Land.

Read Deuteronomy 6:1-2.

1. If the Israelites observed the commands of Scripture, what two results would follow?

2. How do these results challenge the common idea that doing what God commands will ruin your life and make it boring (because you'll let the other guy win or you won't get to fool around sexually)?

Read Deuteronomy 6:3.

3. What does the text say would be the results of being "careful to obey" God?

4. How do these first three verses support the idea that God is *for* us, wanting to produce in us a life that is whole and good in the deepest sense?

Read Deuteronomy 6:4-6.

5. What do the statements in these verses reveal about how we relate to God (especially compared to cultural ideas of legalism and obligation)?

6. Why would love for God and trust in God's motives make us more eager to learn what God thinks about our human life and the way it works ("these commandments")?

Read Deuteronomy 6:7-9.

7. How might day-to-day conversations about God and what God wants for us (decrees, laws and commands) help parents connect with God as well as their children?

"[The Bible] is not only a book which was once spoken, but a book which is now speaking. . . .

If you would follow on to know the Lord, come at once to the open Bible expecting it to speak to you. Do not come with the notion that it is a thing which you can push around at your convenience."

A. W. TOZER

8. What do these verses tell us about letting our life with

God permeate all of our ordinary, mundane activities?

9. How do the truths in verses 1-9 help us know that God is looking for more than a righteousness based only on outward behaviors?

10. Second Timothy 3:16 talks about Scripture as being "God-breathed." How would you describe what God is breathing into us through our reading of Scripture?

"The Bible is the loving heart of God made visible and plain."

Dallas Willard

11. How do you think people who have thoroughly immersed themselves in the wisdom of the Scripture are likely to be different from other folks?

Transformation Exercises

Experiment with one or more of the following.

• Sit in a quiet spot and list situations and locations in your life (committee meeting rooms, relationship with a sister) where your attitude could be transformed by

saying aloud or praying to God silently a passage such
as one of these:

> As the deer pants for streams of water,
>   so my soul pants for you, O God.
> My soul thirsts for God, for the living God.
>   When can I go and meet with God? . . .
> Why are you downcast, O my soul?
>   Why so disturbed within me?
> Put your hope in God,
>   for I will yet praise him,
>   my Savior and my God. (Psalm 42:1-2, 5-6)

- Pretend to be a poet. List some scrumptious, nurtur-
  ing, plentiful images for times of reading Scripture to
  finish this sentence: *Reading Scripture fills me with God
  the way . . .*

  a clear, majestic day of fishing/surfing does

  a lean, flavorful gourmet meal does

  a baby needing to be rocked and finding content-
  ment in your arms does

  a late-night, close-to-the-bone conversation does

  the disciples burned with truth and wisdom on
  the road to Emmaus as Jesus explained things

  other:

- Journal about how much you do and don't trust God to
  do good things in your life. Or make a photo album or

video diary of showing areas in your life where you do trust God and areas where you need to trust him more. Don't be afraid to admit it if you don't trust God that way but would like to.

• Write Psalm 42:1-2, 5-6 on a small card, and memorize it as you jog or walk, letting the psalmist's words linger in your mind as you reflect on them. Careful crossing the roads!

2

READING
AND RESPONDING
TO SCRIPTURE

NEHEMIAH 8:1-18; 9:1-3, 38

*C*ompartmentalized. That word describes how we often approach God's Word. We read it (physical act only); we study and interpret it (intellectual only); we sing it (worship only); we apply it (facing our will only). But the elements of processing Scripture—reading it, studying it, meditating on it, waiting in it, worshiping God, delighting in God, praying it back to God—are all of a piece. For the Israelites the reading of the Law was not a one-mode activity. They put all of themselves into it, and they responded with all of themselves. They *absorbed* it.

Turning Toward God

Picture yourself having just read some verses of Scripture. Which thoughts below characterize your most common response to it? (Circle two or three, if you wish.)

• What in the world did that mean?

• I wish I were as smart as So-and-So; then I could understand this.

• I remember a sermon about this passage—now, what did it say this meant?

• I could never do what this passage commands.

• I wish I could be like that person (or ideal) described in the passage.

• That was new!

• I already knew that!

• That's done. Now it's time to take care of the next thing on my to-do list.

• I'm so sleepy . . .

• Other:

Hearing God Through the Word

Today's passage describes a worship service at a peak moment in Israel's history. The remnant of Judah that returned from Persia not only survived but also rebuilt Jerusalem's walls. They worked hard and trusted God well. And God gave them what they had longed for—they were once again safe in their homeland.

Now it was time to continue their conversation with God, and so the Word was read. Let's look at how they processed Scripture. They set an example for us of letting

God-breathed words interrupt their lives, with the expectation that God would speak to them. They heard and responded in a variety of ways.

Read Nehemiah 8:1-4.

1. Why are the activities described in verse 1 an appropriate response after God had enabled the Jews to rebuild the walls of Jerusalem in just fifty-two days (Nehemiah 1—7)?

2. Describe the listeners and how they listened.

Read Nehemiah 8:5-9.

3. How did the Jews respond to Ezra's opening the book of the Law?

4. What does the example of Ezra and the Levites' "making [the Law] clear" tell us about what we may need to do when reading Scripture?

"We are to pray during our reading so that God might enable us to properly understand himself and his will and open to us one door after the other into his Word."

PHILIPP JAKOB SPENER

5. As the instruction continued, how did the Jews respond (v. 9)?

6. What do these responses from the Jews indicate to you about the importance of expecting to hear from God and responding in some way when Scripture is read?

"Our modern approach to the Word is sometimes characterized by a certain sterility because it relies more on reason than on wisdom, more on speculative study than on participative knowledge, more on thinking than on praying."

ENZO BIANCHI

Read Nehemiah 8:10-18.

7. What did Nehemiah and the Levites urge the people to do instead of to weep? Why was this a good idea?

8. What else did the Jews do in response to the hearing of the Scripture (vv. 14-17)?

Read Nehemiah 9:1-3, 38.

9. In what other ways did the Jews respond to their hearing of Scripture?

10. Which of the following responses to Scripture would you like to try more often? Why?

___ praying

___ worshiping

___ weeping

___ celebrating

___ confessing sin

_____

11. Why is a person who connects with God through Scripture as the Jews did likely to be changed?

"When in reading Scripture you meet with a passage that seems to give your heart a new motion toward God, turn it into the form of a petition, and give it a place in your prayers."

WILLIAM LAW

Transformation Exercises

Experiment with one or more of the following.

• Choose a gesture of response from this passage (such as lifting hands or bowing with your face to the ground, v. 6). As you finish this study, pray to God using that gesture.

• Read Ephesians 1:1-12 aloud slowly. Which word or phrase is most meaningful to you? Why? What does that phrase tell you about how you want to connect with God? If you were to pray phrases from Ephesians 1:1-12 back to God, what would you pray? Here are some starters:

> Open my eyes, O God, to the rich things you're blessing me with that I don't see or understand. (v. 3)

> Thank you, O God, that you loved the idea of me before I was born—even though I tend to think the idea of me is inadequate. (vv. 4-5)

- Journal about the "joy of the Lord" and its relationship to Scripture. Here's an idea to get you started: it is a "joy founded on the feeling of the communion with the Lord, on the consciousness that we have in the Lord a God long-suffering and abundant in goodness and truth."

- Give yourself permission to have a good cry about your relationship with God: how much God loves you; how you may have ignored God; how much God has helped you. Or, in lieu of a cry, go for a walk or run and talk aloud to God.

3

COMPREHENDING
GOD'S TRUTH

ISAIAH 11:1-9

I don't get it" is the phrase we use to indicate that we don't comprehend the meaning of what we read or heard. The purpose of studying the Bible is to "get it." We examine the text carefully to comprehend what the Holy Spirit is communicating through the words on the page. Although the Scripture itself says almost nothing about study, it does urge us to make the effort required to truly hear the Word and follow it, both of which involve comprehension. The goal of studying Scripture is to know God.

Genuine study occurs in many ways. One common method is to ask questions about the text such as these.

1. *Gathering basic facts:* What does this passage say? Who is speaking and who is being spoken to? Based on the historical background, what did the author intend for it to say?

2. *Understanding the text:* What does this passage say about what

God is like? What does it say about human nature? What does it say about how God relates to people?

3. *Applying the text:* What does the passage suggest about how I might pray? What does it suggest about how I might act?

The first set of question helps us collect facts in order to answer the second set, which works toward comprehension (or understanding). We connect the dots between this new information and what we already know. Sometimes the new information makes ideas more clear; other times, it contradicts what we already know and challenges us to think more deeply. The third set of questions helps us reflect on the significance of the passage and ask God to show us how it applies to us.

Turning Toward God

In trying to understand the Bible, what is most helpful to you?

Hearing God Through the Word

The questions below follow the flow of the questions in the introduction. The background for this passage is that Isaiah is speaking to the southern kingdom of Judah, who keeps turning its back on God and is soon to be taken into captivity. Besides warning Judah of this, Isaiah also offers hope about the "shoot" or "Branch" (Jesus) that would come from the "stump of Jesse" (the people who would be left after Judah's captivity and return).

Read Isaiah 11:1-9.

1. What time period(s) does this passage speak about?

   __ Old Testament times

   __ New Testament times

   __ time yet to come

   _____

2. What does Isaiah say that Jesus will be like? (Jesus is referred to as the "shoot" and "Branch.")

   _____

3. What characteristic of Christ (vv. 2-5) is important for you today to help you trust Christ more, so he may "dwell [more fully] in your heart through faith" (Ephesians 3:17)?

   "Study provides a certain objective framework within which meditation can successfully function."

   RICHARD FOSTER

   _____

4. How does Jesus relate to people in this passage, especially verses 3-4?

   _____

5. What do you learn about the Trinity in this passage— God the Father, Jesus the Son and the Holy Spirit (vv. 2-3)?

6. How do the various aspects of the Holy Spirit (mentioned in verse 2 and listed below) equip Jesus to be the righteous and faithful doer of justice described in verses 3-5?

Spirit of wisdom and understanding?

Spirit of counsel and power?

knowledge and fear of the Lord?

---

7. What image (or picture) in this passage is most powerful for you and why?

___ a new twig (Christ) blossoms out of a nearly extinct stump (the remnant of Judah that existed in New Testament times) (v. 1)

___ Jesus' words are so powerful they act as weapons (v. 4)

___ a person (Jesus) so good and devoted that these qualities are fixed in him the way a belt and sash hold clothes on snugly (v. 5)

___ a wolf and a lamb (two natural, habitual foes) are perfectly reconciled (v. 6)

___ a baby is able to play safely with snakes that were deadly on earth (v. 8)

___ another image you find in the passage:

8. Why do you think verses 6-9 are often subtitled "Paradise Regained"?

_____

9. What truth(s) in this passage do you need to absorb more deeply?

_____

10. Consider the truth(s) you mentioned in the previous question. How does it suggest you might pray?

How does it suggest you might act?

_____

11. How do you need to study the Scripture in a more fruitful way?

Transformation Exercises

Experiment with one or more of the following.

- Before listening to a sermon or beginning a Bible study, ask God to give you openness and humility to see how it might contradict what you already believe and what needs to be corrected in your life.

- Choose a Scripture passage (Sermon on the Mount, 1 John, Psalms 145—150) and read it every day for a month. Pay attention to what you learn each day by jotting down a sentence or two about what you noticed each time.

- Examine Matthew 23:23-29 and John 5:39 to find out how the Pharisees and the teachers of the law managed to study the Scripture so well but miss out on what God was saying.

- Look up (in an encyclopedia or art book) the painting *The Peaceable Kingdom* by Edward Hicks, a Pennsylvania Quaker (1780-1849). Behind the Isaiah 11 scene, the background features William Penn and a group of Native Americans making treaties. Penn is paying them for their lands to strengthen relations with them. Ponder this painting for a while, and ask God to show you who a modern-day Edward Hicks would paint alongside you in the background. With whom do you need to reconcile?

4

MEDITATION
AND OBEDIENCE

PSALM 119:97-104

Y ou've probably heard someone say that the longest distance in the world is from a person's head to a person's heart. What that statement usually means is that to know a fact in your mind does not mean you truly believe it in such a way that your behavior changes. The premise behind this Bible study series is that our behavior changes as we connect with God. When we do the connecting, God does the perfecting.

One of the ways we connect with God is through Scripture, but merely reading Scripture or even studying it is not enough. The connection is extended and made stronger as we meditate on Scripture.

The overlooked discipline of meditation on Scripture is mentioned many times in the Bible—fifteen times in Psalms alone. When Scripture talks about meditation, it often mentions obedience in the next breath: "Do not let this Book of the Law depart from your mouth; *meditate* on it day and night, so that you may be *careful to do everything written in it.* Then you will be prosperous and successful" (Joshua 1:8). The one who meditates becomes one who obeys (being careful to do).

Turning Toward God

If God were to wave a magic wand over you and cause a certain fault to disappear, which one would you like for it to be? Grouchiness? Laziness? Procrastination?

Hearing God Through the Word

Psalm 119 connects meditation and obedience. Words such as *meditate, delight* and *heart* (seeking God with all my heart or setting my heart on God's ways) occur often, as do the words *statute, law, decree* and *obey.* God does the perfecting as we meditate on Scripture and then let it resonate in our lives all day long.

Read Psalm 119:97-104.

1. What does the psalmist *do* in relation to the law? How does the psalmist *feel* about the law?

2. How is loving the law different from studying the law?

How are they related?

_____

3. If you were to meditate on God's ideas throughout the
   activities of your day, what activities would lend themselves to ongoing rumination?

_____

4. What advantages does the psalmist find that meditating on the law brings?

"The psalmist in Psalm 119 describes himself as murmuring the Scripture, repeating the texts interiorly, reading the passages of Scripture again and again."

ENZO BIANCHI

_____

5. The phrases "you yourself have taught me" and "how
   sweet are your words to my taste" (vv. 102, 103) indicate the psalmist's personal connectedness with God
   through the text. What, if any, methods of Bible study
   or meditation create that for you?

_____

6. Even though the psalmist writes a lot about obedience, it isn't expressed with a cold-hearted, teeth-

gritting sense of obligation but with great longing for God. How do you explain this?

"It is not that you will think about what you have read, but you will feed upon what you have read. Out of a love for the Lord you exert your will to hold your mind quiet before him. In this peaceful state, swallow what you have tasted . . . take in what is there as nourishment."

JEANNE GUYON

7. Think back to your answer to the "Turning Toward God" question. Why would a person who loved God's law and longed for God think that the fault you mentioned is not a helpful thing to do?

8. Which style(s) of meditation fit(s) best with the way you process life?

___ soaking in and absorbing the meanings of words

___ looking for a word or phrase that speaks to you

___ picturing the ideas expressed or scenes described in the passage

___ enjoying how words are combined (such as *obedience* and *meditation*) and "connecting the dots" between these ideas

___ personalizing words of Scripture with specifics by inserting your own everyday activities ("all day long") or common sins ("every evil path") into the text

___ reading the passage aloud and waiting for a word or phrase to resonate

___ reading it aloud and simply resting or waiting

9. If you were to meditate on a passage and then "pray" it back to God during a time of prayer or even a mundane activity, what passage of Scripture would that be?

---

10. Reread Psalm 119:97-104 aloud slowly. Which phrase stands out to you?

What do you believe God is saying to you today?

"Sit before it and say, 'God, what are you seeking to say to me through this? What is your Word of address to me?'"

ROBERT MULHOLLAND

Transformation Exercises

Experiment with one or more of the following.

• Color-code Psalm 119:97-104 (or all of Psalm 119) according to the following themes. Or use symbols for each theme. You may want to do this on your computer if you can copy the text into a file first.

heart (seeking God with all, setting the heart) = blue or heart shape

law, statutes, decrees, commands, obeying = red
or circle

meditating, delighting = green or triangle

Notice how the themes interrelate, especially how the
psalmist doesn't just "learn" decrees and statutes but delights in them and meditates on them (vv. 16, 23).

• Take a walk, bringing along either a Bible or a printed-
out portion of Scripture. As you walk, put yourself completely into the text and picture yourself as part of it.
For example, put yourself into a Gospel story. Imagine
yourself as

the woman with chronic bleeding who longs for
a secret healing (Mark 5:25-34; add vv. 21-24 for
greater drama)

the father who only half-believes that Jesus can
help his demon-possessed son, but sees Jesus
heal the boy anyway (Mark 9:14-27)

5

A BIBLICAL MODEL

LUKE 1:46-55;
1 SAMUEL 2:1-10

O ne classic method of entering into a Scripture text is called *lectio divina,* which is Latin for "divine reading." Pronounced "lex´-ee-oh di-vee´-nuh," it includes reading a Scripture passage aloud, meditating on it, praying about it and contemplating God in it. As the Bible passage is read, we wait for a word to resonate or "shimmer." Then we meditate on that word or phrase to hear what God might have to say to us. After praying about what this means, we rest in quiet contemplation before God.

The key in *lectio* is to be open to hear God afresh in Scripture. That means setting aside previous ideas of how this passage applies to us. With unfamiliar passages, it may help to do a short preliminary study to understand historical background and individual words so we can open ourselves to hear anew from God. If we are truly open, God usually communicates surprising things we could never have made up ourselves.

Turning Toward God

What is a favorite quote, saying or catch-phrase you like to use that you got from a friend or your grandma or a book? Why does it stick with you?

Hearing God Through the Word

"It is necessary to immerse ourselves in [the Bible], to let it permeate our flesh, to grow so familiar with it that we possess it in the depths of our being and hold it in our memory. A good example is the Magnificat, the Song of Mary. It flows with biblical imagery, clearly the fruit of a heart that knew the Bible."

ENZO BIANCHI

Mary, the mother of Jesus, was a "ponderer." After Jesus' birth and the shepherds' visit she "treasured up all these things and pondered them in her heart" (Luke 2:19). After finding the boy Jesus in Jerusalem engaging in deep discussion with religious leaders, Mary "treasured all these things in her heart" (Luke 2:51). She seems to have been good at meditation.

Read Luke 1:46-55.

1. What key words do you see in this passage?

2. Which phrases, if any, seem particularly wise for a teenage Jewish girl to be singing?

Read 1 Samuel 2:1-10.

3. What themes in this passage are similar to the themes in Luke 1:46-55?

4. In what do both women rejoice?

"The Great Inversion [means that] there are none in the humanly 'down' position so low that they cannot be lifted up by entering God's order, and none in the humanly 'up' position so high that they can disregard God's point of view on their lives. The barren, the widow, the orphan, the eunuch, the alien, all models of human hopelessness, are fruitful and secure in God's care."

DALLAS WILLARD

5. As each woman glorifies God in her song, what qualities of God does each woman mention?

6. People have joked that Mary must have had her Old Testament open to Hannah's song when she sang. How do you explain the similarities?

7. How are the two songs different?

8. How was it possible that Mary could "use" Hannah's song when Mary had not endured similar circumstances (infertility)?

9. Reread Luke 1:47-55 aloud. Which word or phrase emerges from the passage and stays with you?

_____

10. What is it about that word or phrase that draws you?

_____

"We come to the [Bible] text with an openness to hear, to receive, to respond, to be a servant of the Word rather than a master of the text."

ROBERT
MULHOLLAND

11. What might God be calling you to *be* through this word or phrase?

_____

12. Pray silently and ask God what God might be calling you to *do* or *refrain from doing* through your being drawn to this word or phrase. Then wait quietly, enjoying God's presence.

_____

13. In what situation or frame of mind might the word or phrase from this passage be helpful to recall?

Transformation Exercises

Experiment with one or more of the following.

- In a private place, sing a song you know by heart (as Mary probably knew Hannah's song). Sing it several times, and let the words of the song deepen within you. If you know American Sign Language, sign the words as you sing.

- Pick a scriptural phrase you have studied in the past. Rest in it, wait in it and delight in it (but don't analyze it) as you do a physical activity such as mowing the lawn or vacuuming a room.

- Read Genesis 1 and Psalm 8. Compare the ideas and specific words. (Some think Psalm 8 was written as a result of meditating on Genesis 1.) Try meditating on Genesis 1 and writing your own psalm of meditation.

- Pick a passage of Scripture that speaks to you but is not so familiar that it cannot be fresh. Read it aloud to yourself and answer questions 9-13 above.

6

ENTERING A GOSPEL SCENE

MARK 10:17-23

Another common method of meditating on Scripture is to use the imagination and enter the biblical scene as an observer—a fly on the wall or a bystander in the crowd. This common method is explained well in *The Spiritual Exercises of St. Ignatius Loyola*, which urges participants to make use of the five senses. So we imagine what we would see, hear, smell, touch or taste if we had been present in the biblical scene. As we hear the dialogue of the text, we need to let God speak to us, asking us questions, challenging us or comforting us.

This imagination-oriented method is *word*-centered. The exact words of Scripture coach your imagination. Like *lectio divina*, certain words or phrases stand out, but in this method we imagine hearing these words said or saying them ourselves.

Are you reluctant to use your imagination for spiritual growth? C. S. Lewis said that reading George MacDonald's fantasies "converted" or "baptized" his imagination. Let meditating on Scripture baptize yours.

Turning Toward God

When, if ever, has someone confronted you in a loving, genuine way?

Hearing God Through the Word

As you read this text, picture Jesus in conversation with the rich young ruler. Close your eyes. Can you imagine the look on Jesus' face as he loved someone yet challenged him?

Read Mark 10:17-22.

1. How would you describe the manner of the rich young ruler as he approached Jesus?

2. What do you make of Jesus' answer about what a person must do to inherit eternal life?

3. Based on Jesus' behavior and words, what seems to have been in his heart when he replied to the young man (v. 21)?

"Once, the Bible was just so many words to us—'clouds and darkness'—then, suddenly, the words become spirit and life because Jesus re-speaks them to us when our circumstances make the words new."

OSWALD
CHAMBERS

4. What spiritual crisis seems to have occurred within this young man (v. 22)?

Reread Mark 10:17-23 aloud.

5. If you put yourself in the place of the young man as he approaches Jesus, how do you feel as you ask the initial question about inheriting eternal life (v. 17)?

"You seek to allow the text to begin to become that intrusion of the Word of God in to your life, to address you, to encounter you at deeper levels of your being."

ROBERT
MULHOLLAND

6. Try to picture the moment when Jesus answers the young man. What expression do you see on Jesus' face?

What tone do you detect in his voice?

7. Imagine that you're the young man. What does it feel like inside to be invited to be a follower of this great teacher, Jesus, but to be unable to make the choice that will allow you to do so?

8. What is the most stunning thing to you about this passage?

___ Jesus invited the young man to be a follower.

___ Jesus' ability to be unyieldingly firm, but with great love.

___ Jesus' unwillingness to minimize or strike a deal—his insistence that discipleship involves complete reliance on God.

___ Other:

9. What is God saying to you today through this passage?

___ Give up this thing that blocks your reliance on me.

___ Take another small step toward giving up this thing I've asked you to give up many times before.

___ Hear the love in my voice even as I confront you.

___ I still want you as a follower, in spite of . . .

___ You won't know the treasure of heaven here on earth until you've . . .

___ Look at the people around you—they're more important than the physical things you treasure.

___ Other:

"A text may have a different significance or import for me each time I turn to it . . . for the Lord will speak to me where I am."

THELMA HALL

10. How might your relationship with God be affected if you practiced this sort of meditation?

Transformation Exercises

Experiment with one or more of the following.

• Retell your favorite Bible story (to yourself if no one else), but put yourself in the main character's place and tell it as if it were about you.

• Read Luke 13:10-13 and act it out. Take the role of the main character and imagine you've been crippled for eighteen years. You're sitting in the synagogue, completely bent over, listening to the teacher. Get up and walk bent over at least eighteen steps—one for every year. Walk to the front of the synagogue bent over (the length of a large room) as Jesus calls you forward. Hear Jesus' voice free you from your infirmity. Feel Jesus' hands on you, releasing it. Straighten up and praise God. What do you say? How do you feel?

• Journal about the idea of your imagination's being baptized. How could this save you from repeated sins? How could this change your behavior?

GUIDELINES FOR LEADERS

My grace is sufficient for you. (2 Corinthians 12:9)

If leading a small group is something new for you, don't worry. These sessions are designed to be led easily. Because the Bible study questions flow from observation to interpretation to application, you may feel as if the studies lead themselves.

You don't need to be an expert on the Bible or a trained teacher to lead a small group discussion. As a leader, you can guide group members to discover for themselves what the Bible has to say and to listen for God's guidance. This method of learning will allow group members to remember much more of what is said than a lecture would.

This study guide is flexible. You can use it with a variety of groups—students, professionals, neighborhood or church folks. Each study takes forty-five to sixty minutes in a group setting.

It's true that getting people to discuss the Bible requires some thought. The suggestions listed below will help you encourage discussion by paying attention to group dynamics.

Preparing for the Study

1. Ask God to help you understand and apply the passage in your own life. Unless this happens, you will not be prepared to lead others. Pray too for the various members of the group. Ask God to open your hearts to the message and motivate you to action.

2. Read the introduction to the entire guide to get an overview of the issues that will be explored.

3. As you begin each study, read and reread the assigned Scripture passage to familiarize yourself with it. Read also the focus statement at the beginning of the notes for that study, which appear later in this section.

4. This study guide is based on the New International Version of the Bible. It will help you and the group if you use this translation as the basis for your study and discussion.

5. Carefully work through each question in the study. Spend time in meditation and reflection as you consider how to respond.

6. Write your thoughts and responses in the space provided in the study guide. This will help you to express your understanding of the passage clearly.

7. It may help to have a Bible dictionary handy. Use it to look up any unfamiliar words, names or places. (For additional help on how to study a passage, see *How to Lead a LifeGuide Bible Study* from InterVarsity Press.)

8. Consider how you need to apply the Scripture to your life. Remember that the group members will follow your lead in responding to the studies. They will not go any deeper than you do.

Leading the Study

1. Begin the study on time. Open with prayer, asking God to help the group to understand and apply the passage.

2. Be sure that everyone in your group has a study guide. There are some questions and activities they will need to work through on their own before, during or after the study session.

3. At the beginning of your first session together, explain that these studies are meant to be discussions, not lectures. Encourage the members of the group to participate. However, do not put pressure on those who may be hesitant to speak during the first few sessions. You may want to suggest

the following guidelines to your group.

- Stick to the topic being discussed.

- Base your response on the verses studied, not on outside authorities such as commentaries or speakers.

- Focus on the passage of Scripture studied. Only rarely should you refer to other portions of the Bible. This allows for everyone to participate on equal ground and for in-depth study.

- Anything said in the group is considered confidential and will not be discussed outside the group unless specific permission is given to do so.

- Help everyone get involved by limiting your responses if you contribute a lot or by responding more if you're usually quiet. But don't feel forced to speak up.

- Listen attentively to each other and learn from one another.

- Pray for each other, especially if you feel that someone is struggling with an answer. Praying is better than interrupting.

4. Have a group member read aloud the introduction at the beginning of the discussion.

5. Every session begins with a "Turning Toward God" section. The questions or activities are meant to be used before the passage is read. These questions introduce the theme of the study and encourage group members to begin to open up. Encourage as many members as possible to participate, and be ready to get the discussion going with your own response.

6. Have one or more group member(s) read aloud the passage to be studied.

7. As you ask the questions under "Hearing God Through the Word," keep in mind that they are designed to be used just as they are written. You may simply read them aloud. Or you may prefer to express them in your own words.

There may be times when it is appropriate to deviate from the study guide. For example, a question may have already been answered. If so, move on to the next question. Or someone may raise an important question not covered in the guide. Take time to discuss it, but try to keep the group from going off on tangents.

8. Avoid answering your own questions. If necessary repeat or rephrase them until they are clearly understood. Or point out something you read in the leader's notes to clarify the context or meaning. An eager group quickly becomes passive and silent if members think the leader will do most of the talking.

9. Don't be afraid of silence in response to the discussion questions. People may need time to think about the question before formulating their answers. Count to twenty before rephrasing or commenting.

10. Don't be content with just one answer. Ask, "What do the rest of you think?" or "Anything else?" until several people have given answers to the question.

11. Acknowledge all contributions. Try to be affirming whenever possible. Never reject an answer. If it is clearly off-base, ask, "Which verse led you to that conclusion?" or again, "What do the rest of you think?"

12. Don't expect every answer to be addressed to you, even though this will probably happen at first. As group members become more at ease, they will begin to truly interact with each other. This is one sign of healthy discussion.

13. Don't be afraid of controversy. It can be very stimulating. If you don't resolve an issue completely, don't be frustrated. Explain that the group will move on and God may enlighten group members in later sessions.

14. Periodically summarize what the group has said about the passage. This helps to draw together the various ideas mentioned and gives continuity to the study. But don't preach.

15. Every session ends with "Transformation Exercises." At the end of the study, have a participant read them aloud. Then ask each participant to choose the one that fits them best, according to their personality or current needs. Ask them to tell the group which one that is and a time they could try it.

    Before the next session starts, ask whether any participants tried the transformation exercises. You might lead into this by telling about one you tried. So-called failures really are not failures. These things are a matter of skill building. You never learn to ride a bike unless you get on it the first time and keep trying.

16. Conclude your time together with conversational prayer, adapting the prayer suggestion at the end of the study to your group. Ask for God's help in following through on the commitments you've made.

17. End on time.

Many more suggestions and helps can be found in *The Big Book on Small Groups* (from InterVarsity Press).

STUDY NOTES

Session 1. Immersing Yourself in God's Thoughts
Deuteronomy 6:1-9

Focus: We need to become thoroughly familiar with Scripture, not just for the sake of knowledge but to connect with God and be coached by God on how to live a life of wholeness. This won't happen, however, unless we trust that God genuinely loves us and that scriptural commands are the keys to the best possible life on earth.

Question 1. They would fear the Lord and enjoy long life. This helps us see that knowledge of Scripture is not a goal in itself but God's coaching for wise living. *Coaching* is an appropriate word because God comes alongside us in Scripture, offering instruction, models and encouragement.

Question 2. We struggle to believe that God offers us the best possible life, of a sort of goodness that is appealing. The enemy of our soul convinces us that God is a killjoy, when God is actually the giver of real joy. Obeying God isn't difficult: Scripture helps us connect with God, and so the "burden is light."

Question 3. Things would go well with them, and their lives would flow with untold benefits in the Promised Land.

Question 4. With a holy, healthy fear of God (v. 2), we look to God as the One who loves us completely and holds the keys to the transformed life. Observing God's commands wipes away the falseness we gravitate toward and leads us to live in wholeness. God's commands teach us how to build genuine relationships with others. They do not lead to a horrible life of depriving ourselves of the goodies we want.

Question 5. God was not like the false Canaaanite gods who required capricious acts of worship (such as sacrificing children). Verse 5 makes it clear that the Old Testament is not a collection of rules with no emphasis on relationship with God. Obedience is not found in constantly focusing on self and behavioral failures but in thoroughly immersing oneself in God: heart, soul and strength. Says J. A. Thompson, "Obedience was not to spring from a barren legalism based on necessity and duty. It was to arise from a relationship based on love."[1]

Question 6. To obey God in a full-hearted way requires a belief that God can be trusted to meet our needs, to care for us, not to do us harm. We need to trust that we're not going to need to lie or commit adultery to get our needs met. If we truly believe God has what we need and can meet our needs, we're more eager to read Scripture.

Question 7. Talking about God to a child can help adults simplify difficult concepts such as omnipotence and atonement and focus on basic but central truths (God loves you, God wants you to love and obey). This thinking process helps parents as well as children.

Question 8. Constant exposure to God's words creates an ongoing conversation between God and the reader. God becomes "the subject of conversation both inside and outside the home, from the beginning of the day to the end of the day. . . . The commandments were to permeate every sphere of the life of man."[2] We begin to trust that God speaks to us regularly through the Word.

Question 9. Obedience flows from the central motive and activity: to

---

[1] J. A. Thompson, *Deuteronomy,* Tyndale Old Testament Commentaries (Downers Grove, Ill.: InterVarsity Press, 1976), p. 122.
[2] Peter C. Craigie, *The Book of Deuteronomy,* New International Commentary on the Old Testament (Grand Rapids, Mich.: Eerdmans, 1976), p. 170.

love God with everything you've got. It involves having the textured heart of a deeply good person.

Question 10. God is transforming our souls, "draw[ing] men into Christ, to make them little Christs,"[3] to make people the "same kind of thing as himself."[4]

Question 11. Because they're coming to know God, they are developing a deep-down wisdom and goodness, void of pretension or religiosity.

Session 2. Reading and Responding to Scripture
Nehemiah 8:1-18; 9:1-3, 38

Focus: When Scripture is read, we respond in many ways, including prayer, worship, weeping, celebrating and confessing sin.

Turning Toward God. Keep this lighthearted with your own answers, such as imitating how we fall asleep or try to remember what a favorite radio preacher said.

Hearing God Through the Word. If reading aloud, you may say the first letter of the names in verses 4 and 7 instead of trying to pronounce them.

Question 1. The Jews had experienced God as their helper. This made them hungry for more of God and more anxious to discover how to live as God prescribed.

Question 2. This group included men, women and anyone who could understand—probably older children. They listened attentively.

Question 3. See verse 6. They stood up. They lifted their hands. They bowed their heads and worshiped with faces on the ground. They *responded*—they seem to have been praying.

Question 4. Ezra and the Levites seem to have offered explanations of Scripture, but "making it clear" also included translating it for those who

---

[3]C. S. Lewis, *Mere Christianity* (New York: Macmillan, 1970), p. 169.
[4]Ibid., p. 162.

spoke only Aramaic. They set an example of diligence in Scripture reading, or "rightly dividing the word of truth" (2 Timothy 2:15).

To help make Scripture clear to ourselves, we may need to examine the background of a passage and compare it with other passages to understand the "whole counsel of God" (Acts 20:27 NKJV). Using a commentary and reading parallel passages are helpful. Noticing the theme of the passage and how each verse relates to that are very important.

This passage will show that studying Scripture is an important preliminary activity, serving the goal of knowing God and interacting with this living God. Then I open the Bible with anticipation that God is going to impart to me today what I need to know.

Question 5. They wept. They experienced what is described in Hebrews 4:12: "For the word of God is living and active. Sharper than any double-edged sword, it penetrates even to dividing soul and spirit, joints and marrow; it judges the thoughts and attitudes of the heart."

Question 6. To read Scripture without this expectation is to neglect to let these God-breathed words interrupt our lives so that God can teach us, rebuke us, correct us and train us (2 Timothy 3:16).

Question 7. Nehemiah urged them to celebrate, but this was not mere revelry but a "joy founded on the feeling of the communion with the Lord, on the consciousness that we have in the Lord a God long-suffering and abundant in goodness and truth."[5] The Levites urged them to "be still" as in Psalm 46:10, "Be still, and know that I am God."

Any time people understand "the words made known to them" in Scripture (v. 12), a dramatic response such as this celebration is appropriate. Scriptural clarity challenges our will, and we need to respond. The consequences of not doing so are described in the old saying "Impression without expression causes depression."

---

[5]C. F. Keil, *Commentary on the Old Testament,* vol. 3, *I and II Kings, I and II Chronicles, Ezra, Nehemiah, Esther* (Grand Rapids, Mich.: Eerdmans, 1973), p. 232.

Question 8. These returned exiles built booths and lived in them, cele-brating the Feast of Booths as it had not been celebrated since the time of Joshua. This feast was a harvest festival, commemorating the beginning of the forty years of wandering in the wilderness (Exodus 23:16). During the festival, people lived in tents or booths in Jerusalem to remind themselves of how their ancestors lives as they wandered. However, it was a joyous fes-tival, full of games and dancing.

Question 9. They confessed their sins and worshiped God. They made written agreements with each other about how they would behave in the fu-ture. It's as if they said, "What I heard leads me to do . . . Help me." In *Praying the Word* Enzo Bianchi advises, "You should make some practical resolutions which are based on your state in life and your position in society, always al-lowing the Word to be the guiding force in your life."[6]

Question 10. Someone might protest that these must be spontaneous and cannot be planned. But they can be deliberate responses to Scripture. Weep-ing or celebration may not come automatically, but we can journal about rea-sons the Scripture we read might make us want to weep or celebrate.

Question 11. Back-and-forth conversation with God through Scripture reading builds a relationship that changes a person where simple efforts to obey commands will not.

Session 3. Comprehending God's Truth
Isaiah 11:1-9

Focus: We study Scripture to comprehend what the Holy Spirit is com-municating through it to give us a better knowledge of God.

Turning Toward God. Ask which methods or attitudes or settings help most. Be open to ideas other than those in the introduction. Because people have different styles of learning, different approaches work, such as analyt-

---

[6]Enzo Bianchi, *Praying the Word* (Kalamazoo, Mich.: Cistercian Publications, 1998), p. 81.

ical methods of Bible study; reading commentaries; interacting with others to stimulate thinking; simple, common-sense approaches taken by a particular speaker or a series of studies; coming up with hunches from a passage and following up with other passages to see if those hunches are true; connecting truth in Scripture to truth in art and literature.

Question 1. All three. Isaiah is speaking to Judah in Old Testament times about their upcoming captivity. His message is about Jesus' appearance in New Testament times and about time everlasting—the "peaceable kingdom" of heaven (vv. 6-9).

Question 2. The Spirit of the Lord will rest on Jesus and Jesus will delight in the fear of the Lord. Jesus will not be fooled by outward appearances but will judge with integrity based on righteousness and faithfulness.

Question 4. (This question begins the second cycle of observe, interpret and apply questions.) Jesus looks on the heart, not outward appearances (1 Samuel 16:7). The word translated "judge" in verse 4 is better understood as "do justice to." The poor and the humble—who do not "catch a break"—will finally get the help and respect they need. (Studying the meaning of words in their original language can help us.)

The odd picture in the last phrase of verse 4 is understood better when we remember who is speaking. Prophets such as Isaiah spoke to distracted people. They were not listened to, so they often used arresting, even odd, word pictures to get listeners' attention. Isaiah referred to Jesus' words and breath, though not physical entities, as being so strong they would be capable of punishment and death.

Question 5. The Spirit rests on Jesus who then delights in but stands in awe of God the Father. You might ask participants if this enlightens or contradicts their current understanding of the Trinity. Honest study requires that we remain open to the Scriptures contradicting what we already know or think. Reconciling seeming contradictions often helps us think more clearly and understand more of God's infinite greatness.

Question 6. Here are some ideas:

What Jesus is like	This equips Jesus to be
Spirit of wisdom and understanding	guide for his people
Spirit of counsel and power	guardian for his people
knowledge and fear of the Lord	example for his people

Question 9. Here are some ideas:

- God brings redemption and reconciliation (Jesus) out of failure (the remnant of Judah)

- the community of the Trinity: the Spirit interacts with Jesus in the fear of God (v. 2)

- God judges not by outward appearance but with true rightness and justice

- in the kingdom of God, bitter enemies (including those in the animal world) no longer have fierce conflicts but live together peaceably

Transformation Exercises. Encourage participants to try all of them. The second exercise is helpful for those who learn better through repetition rather than asking formal questions. The third one is for those who love looking for clues and drawing conclusions. The last exercise may help those who are more visual or imaginative or who love comparisons.

Session 4.
Meditation and Obedience
Psalm 119:97-104

Focus: Because meditation on Scripture is one more way to connect with God, it leads to obedience.

Turning Toward God. Confess a fault or two of your own to get them started. If you wish, lighten up the tone first by rewording the question to end with, "what fault would your mother or your spouse or your roommate like for it to be?"

Question 1. You may wonder what "the law" is that we love and meditate on. "The law" refers to the Ten Commandments, but "the entire law is summed up in a single command: Love your neighbor as yourself'" (Galatians 5:14). New Testament passages such as the Sermon on the Mount (Matthew 5—7), Colossians 3:1-17 and Romans 12:9-21 explain the nitty-gritty of the law—how to become the kind of person who obeys the law—not placing anything before God, not taking God's name in vain, not murdering people even in our thoughts.

If someone protests that Christians are not "under the law," explain that Christ's coming, death and resurrection fulfilled the law but did not abolish it. Although we are *justified* by grace (not the law), the law is now a pathway to grace through the Holy Spirit. Paul's words in Romans 7:22 resemble Psalm 119:97: "For in my inner being I delight in God's law."

What we avoid is trying to be justified by law-keeping or being self-righteous about obeying God's commands (Galatians 5:4, Luke 11:52). If further discussion is required, set aside another time to look at Romans 7:4-12, 8 and Galatians 3, 5.

Question 2. Having studied the law and found a treasure, one loves it by thinking about it and giving up everything else to bask in it. (Consider the parable of the man who found the treasure buried in the field and gave up everything to have it. How he must have pondered it! Imagined himself owning it! Thought about how wonderful the treasure was! Wondered that he was going to own it himself!) Loving the law is like this. It is worth the time to bask in a Scripture and taste and see that the Lord is good.

Question 3. Physical activities, especially walking, running, riding a bike or gardening, are excellent. In fact, you can train yourself to do this by doing these activities after you spend time soaking in the Word and loving it. Sometimes relatively mindless activities work well—running errands, mowing the lawn, washing dishes.

Question 5. If few participants have an answer, ask if any have experienced connecting with God through Scripture and, if so, to tell about it.

Question 6. Meditation is a very relational discipline in which you give yourself—your imagination and inner brooding—to God. God can use that part of yourself to teach you to long for all that God is.

Question 7. You might want to mention that someone who loves God's law is convinced that God's principles for goodness are not only to be cherished (v. 103) but also give exceptional wisdom.

Question 9. Encourage participants to choose passages they've recently studied and understood. Or familiar passages (the Lord's Prayer, Psalm 23) can be excellent.

Question 10. Offer to read the passage aloud at this time and let participants rest in the passage and then write their answers. Allow at least seven to ten minutes.

Session 5.
A Biblical Model
Luke 1:46-55; 1 Samuel 2:1-10

Focus: What comes out of our mouths is a result of what we meditate on. This seems to have happened to Mary in her song that flowed from Hannah's song. The *lectio divina* method helps us follow Mary's example.

Question 1. Before the passage is read, you may wish to do two things.

1. Point out that Mary sang this song when she was pregnant with Jesus. She had gone to visit her cousin Elizabeth, and after Elizabeth called her "mother of the my Lord" (v. 43) she responded with this song.

2. Read this first question so that participants can listen for themes as the Scripture is read.

The question is for brainstorming purposes only. Write down the themes that are mentioned for use later. After the question is read, ask the group to hold their place in Luke 1.

Question 3. Before the passage is read, you may wish to note that this is a song sung by Hannah, a previously infertile woman who asked God for a son and later gave birth to Samuel.

Question 5. Mary sings that God's name is holy (v. 49). Hannah says no one is holy like God (v. 2). She also says that God is unique and a rock. They are both marveling at God's initiative and God's actions, which demonstrate God's power.

Question 6. Many believe Mary was singing from her heart based on what had been cultivated there through meditating on Hannah's song. (Mary also borrows phrases from several psalms, including Psalm 138:6; 71:19; 111:9; 103:17; 98:1; 107:9; 98:3; 132:11.) Noting the similarities between the women's songs, commentator Norval Geldenhuys writes, "All pious Israelites from their childhood days knew by heart songs from the Old Testament and often sang them in the home circle and at celebrations. Mary was steeped in the poetical literature of her nation, and accordingly her hymn also bears the unmistakable signs of it."[7]

Question 7. Geldenhuys points out, "While Mary sings her happiness with deep humility and holy reserve, Hannah completely surrenders herself to a feeling of personal triumph over her enemies. Where Mary borrowed expressions from the Old Testament, she gives to the consecrated words a deep meaning and higher application."[8]

Question 8. Although Mary's situation was different, she identified with many of the scriptural truths expressed in Hannah's song. When Scripture has been meditated upon and "written in the heart," it has personal meaning and can be transferred and personalized to many situations.

Question 9. Before reading the passage aloud, ask participants to shut their eyes. If you wish, read aloud the Mulholland quote on page 38. To benefit especially the men in the group, preface the reading by saying something about how this passage can be a song for women *and* men who have had no

[7]Norval Geldenhuys, *The Gospel of Luke,* New International Commentary on the New Testament (Grand Rapids, Mich.: Eerdmans, 1977), p. 85.
[8]Ibid.

reason to think God would choose to use them in any way.

Then have the passage read aloud slowly, with equal weight given to each word. Urge participants to wait quietly in the silence afterward to see what word resonates or shimmers. You may want to add this idea from Robert Mulholland: "You may find yourself in a 'holding pattern' on just one sentence [or one word]."[9]

After a few minutes, ask them to share that word with the group.

Question 10. Urge participants to close their eyes again and ponder.

Question 12. Allow several minutes of quiet so that participants may pray and have a few moments of contemplation. Then ask them to open their eyes and prepare themselves to discuss the next question.

Question 13. Explain that not all participants will have an answer. We sometimes understand the importance of a word or phrase only by waiting on God for a longer period of time, maybe even a few days.

Session 6. Entering a Gospel Scene
Mark 10:17-23

Focus: The detailed scene of the rich young ruler is ideal for the Ignatian sort of meditation, using the imagination. We can jump into the scene and let Jesus speak directly to us.

Turning Toward God. When we're confronted, it's often in a mean-spirited tone. But a loving confrontation can have a transforming effect on us.

Question 1. He ran up to meet Jesus with enthusiasm even though Jesus was "on his way." He fell before him, which would indicate one of two things. Either he truly adored Jesus from watching him and hearing him, or he was being obsequious and fawning, making a big fuss over Jesus. Commentator Will Lane chooses the former: "The eager approach of a man while Jesus was setting out on his way, his kneeling posture, the formal address together with

---

[9]Robert Mulholland, *Shaped by the Word* (Nashville: Upper Room, 2000), p. 55.

the weighty character of his question—all suggest deep respect for Jesus and genuine earnestness on the part of the man himself."[10] (Parallel passages tell us the man was young [Matthew 19:20] and a ruler [Luke 18:18].)

Question 2. Jesus was not at odds with the law. He saw in the Old Testament law the key components of discipleship. Jesus seems to be drawing the man forward by appealing to the law, with which the young man is quite familiar. He is putting his finger on the man's hunger.

If someone comments on Jesus' refusal to accept the descriptor *good,* you might reply with this clarification by Will Lane: "In the Old Testament and subsequent Judaism only God is characteristically called 'good,' although it was possible to speak in a derived sense of 'the good man' (Prov. 12:2; 14:14, others)."[11]

Question 3. Jesus' look of love communicates that he had a tender heart of love and that he was skilled at speaking the truth in love (Ephesians 4:15). Also, Jesus must have had a high opinion of the young man, since he invited him to become a follower! Still, Jesus was tough, insisting the young man would have to do what the Twelve had done—abandon everything to follow him.

Question 4. Initially so eager to please Jesus, he was giving up the invitation to become a follower because he couldn't let go of something he loved more. No wonder his face fell. Says Hugh Anderson: "Since this man is captive to what the world has offered him he is not free to receive God's offer [of discipleship], vexed though he is to say No to it."[12]

Question 5. Before reading the passage aloud (even if you're doing the study by yourself), explain that the previous three questions helped the group study the basic words and ideas of the text. Now it's time to read the text again and *enter into* it.

---

[10]William Lane, *The Gospel According to Mark,* New International Commentary on the New Testament (Grand Rapids, Mich.: Eerdmans, 1975), p. 364.

[11]Ibid.

[12]Hugh Anderson, *The Gospel of Mark,* New Century Bible Commentary (Grand Rapids, Mich.: Eerdmans, 1981), p. 250.

If you wish, ask participants to shut their eyes and imagine themselves as this young man before they answer. He seems to have been very confident: "The inquirer's idea of goodness was defined by human achievement. He regarded himself as 'good' in that he had fulfilled the commandments. . . . Now he hopes to discover from another 'good' man what he can do to assure eternal life."[13]

If you have time after answering this question, ask participants to put themselves in the place of some disciples standing by. Are they embarrassed by this boy's kneeling or his bold interruption?

Question 6. Participants will need to close their eyes to picture an expression on Jesus' face based on the words of the text. The words *loved him* "may denote either that [Jesus] openly showed affection by putting his arms around him or had the profoundest sympathy for his need."[14] A certain earnestness in Jesus is appropriate too, given that he invites the young man to be one of his followers.

Question 7. Suggest that participants try letting their own faces move from expressions of eagerness to disappointment to see how that facial movement affects them inside. It must have been an episode of roller-coaster emotions: first the youth's intense enthusiasm and devotion, then his disappointment.

Question 9. Ask participants to close their eyes. Explain that you're going to read the passage aloud to them once more, then ask the question. Urge them not to jump at an easy answer or feel as if they have to make something up. When we sit quietly before God, God often has surprising things to say to us. They may want to ask themselves: *What question is God asking me through this text?*

After you've asked the question and waited a few minutes, ask participants to share their answers. If "nothing" came to them, that's fine. The quiet provided them a moment to simply enjoy the presence of God.

---

[13]Lane, *Gospel According to Mark,* p. 365.
[14]Anderson, *Gospel of Mark,* p. 249.

SOURCES

Introduction

Henri Nouwen, *Making All Things New* (San Francisco: HarperSanFrancisco, 1981), p. 66.

Chart content taken from Jan Johnson, *Listening to God* (Colorado Springs: NavPress, 1997).

Session 1

SIDEBARS

A. W. Tozer, *The Pursuit of God* (Camp Hill, Penn.: Christian Publications, 1982), pp. 81-82.

Dallas Willard, unpublished manuscript.

Session 2

SIDEBARS

Philipp Jakob Spener, "The Necessary and Useful Reading of the Holy Scriptures," quoted in *The Spiritual Formation Bible, NRSV* (Grand Rapids, Mich.: Zondervan, 1999), p. 925.

Enzo Bianchi, *Praying the Word* (Kalamazoo, Mich.: Cistercian Publications, 1998), p. 23.

William Law, *A Serious Call to a Devout and Holy Life* (London: J. Richardson, 1720), p. 200, as quoted in *Spiritual Formation Bible*, p. 670.

TRANSFORMATION EXERCISE THREE

C. F. Keil, *Commentary on the Old Testament*, vol. 3, *I and II Kings, I and II Chronicles, Ezra, Nehemiah, Esther* (Grand Rapids, Mich.: Eerdmans, 1973), p. 232.

Session 3

INTRODUCTION

J. Steven Harper, "Meeting God in Scripture," in *The Spiritual Formation Bible, NRSV* (Grand Rapids, Mich.: Zondervan, 1999), p. 1089.

SIDEBARS

Richard Foster, *Celebration of Discipline* (San Francisco: Harper & Row, 1988), p. 64.

QUESTION SEVEN
Franz Delitzsch, *Commentary on the Old Testament,* vol. 7, *Biblical Commentary on the Prophecies of Isaiah* (Grand Rapids, Mich.: Eerdmans, 1969), 1:284.

Session 4
SIDEBARS
Enzo Bianchi, *Praying the Word* (Kalamazoo, Mich.: Cistercian Publications, 1998), p. 50.
Jeanne Guyon, *Experiencing the Depths of Jesus Christ* (Beaumont, Tex.: SeedSowers, 1975), p. 11.
Robert Mulholland, *Shaped by the Word* (Nashville: Upper Room, 2000), p. 57.

Session 5
SIDEBARS
Enzo Bianchi, *Praying the Word* (Kalamazoo, Mich.: Cistercian Publications, 1998), p. 52.
Dallas Willard, *The Divine Conspiracy* (San Francisco: HarperSanFrancisco, 1998), pp. 88-89.
Robert Mulholland, *Shaped by the Word* (Nashville: Upper Room, 2000), p. 57.

Session 6
INTRODUCTION
C. S. Lewis, introduction to George MacDonald, *Phantastes* (Grand Rapids, Mich.: Eerdmans, 2000), p. xi.

SIDEBARS
Oswald Chambers, *My Utmost for His Highest,* updated ed., ed. James Reimann (Grand Rapids, Mich.: Discovery House, 1992), January 3 entry.
Robert Mulholland, *Shaped by the Word* (Nashville: Upper Room, 2000), p. 56.
Thelma Hall, *Too Deep for Words: Rediscovering Lectio Divina* (New York: Paulist, 1988), p. 37.

TRANSFORMATION EXERCISE TWO
This and other intriguing ideas are included in Anne Broyles, *Journaling: A Spirit Journey* (Nashville: Upper Room, 1988), pp. 45-46.

For more information on Jan Johnson's writing and speaking ministry, visit **<www.janjohnson.org>**.
Or contact Jan at 4897 Abilene St., Simi, CA 93063